The God-Madness

First published in 2008 by
Dedalus Press
13 Moyclare Road
Baldoyle
Dublin 13
Ireland

www.dedaluspress.com

ISBN 978 1 904556 86 2

Dedalus Press titles are represented in North America
by Syracuse University Press, Inc., 621 Skytop Road,
Suite 110, Syracuse, New York 13244,
and in the UK by Central Books,
99 Wallis Road, London E9 5LN.

Typesetting/Design: Pat Boran
Cover image © Marco Testa

Printed and bound in the UK by Lightning Source,
6 Precedent Drive, Rooksley, Milton Keynes MK13 8PR, UK.

The Dedalus Press receives financial assistance from
An Chomhairle Ealaíon / The Arts Council, Ireland

The God-Madness

a selection from the Lauds of
Jacopone da Todi

translated from the Italian by
Pádraig J. Daly

Contents

۔۔

Preface

The selection of poems that I have translated in this volume may give a slightly lopsided view of Jacopone da Todi. It contains none of his slaughterous fulminations against Pope Boniface VIII nor any of his invective-rich, political and homiletic tirades. It concentrates instead on the poems that interest me most, a small sampling of his later 'Lauds'. I love them inordinately for their enviable certainties about God, their insight into Love and their flamboyant and, sometimes, heartbreaking drama.

As a member of another Religious Order which emerged from the same 13th century Umbro-Tuscan ferment, I feel that Jacopone is not someone I'd have cared to live in community with. I'd have found his zeal for Franciscan simplicity extreme. At the same time, I would have, I hope, hugely admired his moral courage and integrity.

As his name implies, Jacopone was born in the Umbrian hilltop town of Todi, in the year 1230. His family was wealthy. At an early age, he married the beautiful Vanna. (All women who die young are reputed beautiful). When she died, early in their marriage, when a roof collapsed at a banquet, he found that she wore a penitential hairshirt beneath her gorgeous ballgown. This spurred him, firstly, to become a public penitent, and then, after a period of extremely eccentric behaviour, to enter the recently formed Order of Friars Minor of St. Francis of Assisi.

The Franciscans were fiercely divided at the time; and Jacopone threw in his lot with the (often fanatical) Spirituals in their controversy with the more relaxed and, perhaps, more worldly Conventual Friars. He eventually fell foul of Pope Boniface VIII, whom he didn't in any case recognise as pope, and was excommunicated and jailed for siding with the Colonnas against him. The excommunication was withdrawn by Pope Benedict XI, when Jacopone was in his seventies. He was freed from prison and resumed his life as a friar. It was in this period, it seems, that he composed these poems of empathy with the Suffering Saviour, of joy and of exultation.

Like George Herbert in England, Jacopone was filled with the conviction that God extravagantly loves sinful humans. Jacopone is, however, more word-prodigal than Herbert and his extrovert, singing voice is unmistakably that of early Franciscan Umbria. He is a master of dramatic dialogue. His wonderful 'Laud 93' enters into the predicament of Jesus in Calvary through the eyes of Mary and the other onlookers. This may have been what led people to ascribe the medieval Latin masterpiece 'Stabat Mater' to Jacopone. If he didn't write it, he certainly was very close to its spirit. I once had the fortune to hear a setting of the 'Stabat Mater' sung in Todi Cathedral. Nobody there had any doubt as to its being the work of a local boy.

Few people nowadays would subscribe completely to Jacopone's theological outlook. Jacopone did not have the insights of modern theology or scripture studies. 'The Lauds' celebrate madness for the sake of Christ and sometimes Jacopone appears barely to cling to the right side of sanity, not to talk of orthodoxy. But how can anyone express religious experience without destroying it?

As for these translations—Here I give hostages to fortune! —they are inadequate; and at times appear to me utterly pedestrian when I place them beside the melodious originals.

But hopefully they capture just a little of the flavour of Jacopone, insofar as English is open to such work. Modem Irish, I have found, is far more hospitable to Italian exuberance. Translating Jacopone was difficult in so many ways. I agonised over single words and phrases and sometimes had to settle for English words that only partially conveyed the Italian, choosing what seemed to me to be the most important nuance over many other possibilities. And I found no way at all around Jacopone's punning, e.g. the regular punning of "amo", meaning "fishhook" with "amo", meaning "I love". I do hope, however, that I have opened up something of Jacopone's ebullient spirit to the chance reader of this small sampling. Maybe, too, these translations will lead some readers towards the madness they celebrate.

Pádraig J. Daly

The God-Madness

LAUD 75

A Dialogue about the Cross

"I FLEE THE CROSS which eats me up:
I cannot abide its warmth.

"I cannot take heat so intense
As that which the cross throws out: I flee from love.
Refuge there is none since I carry in my heart
A memory that consumes me."

"Why run, Brother, from an object so delightful?
As for me, I seek it out:
You are a fool
To spurn such enjoyment."

"I flee, Brother, because I am wounded:
The blow has fallen and split open my heart:
You cannot be feeling as I feel:
None of what you say describes it."

"Brother, what I know is a cross in blossom:
I have wrapped myself in its contemplation.
It does me no injury:
Wallowing in it is my joy."

"For my part, it is a volley of arrows
That lodge in my heart:
The archer has taken aim
And cut through my armour."

"I was blind but now I see the light
All from gazing at the cross:
It guides me and leads me merrily on;
I am in misery away from it."

"As for me, the light has bedazzled me
Bringing such brightness
That I am as the blind man
Whose eyes, though beautiful, gaze emptily."

"I can speak, who once was dumb,
All because I have seen the cross:
I need to tell everyone
Of the nourishment it gives."

"I who was a prattler am now struck dumb:
My heart has entered so deep an abyss
That no one who listens
Can comprehend me."

"Once I was dead, now I am living
All because of the cross's appearing:
I expire when it leaves me,
Revive at its return."

"I am not dead yet, but draw my final gasps
(God will, the end be quick!)
I am in constant extremity
And cannot cut loose."

"Brother, the cross is my delight;
Don't witter on about its torment.
Maybe, you are not in harmony at all
With the Spouse you would embrace."

"You are in the heat, I am in the fire:
For you there is delight, for me only roasting.
I can find no refuge from the burning.
From outside, how can you comprehend?"

"Brother, you speak of your flight from love
In ways beyond me.
I would know more
If you could but address my heart."

"You enjoy the first draught;
But I, having drunk deep, cannot be content with must.
Nowhere is there a hoop so strong
That my ferment does not rupture it."

LAUD 76

The Exultation of the Heart

O EXULTATION OF THE HEART, making us sing
love songs!

When the exultation takes hold, it sets us singing:
The tongue begins to babble, knowing not what to utter;
Joy so overpowering cannot be covered.

When the exultation is aflame, our tongues are screaming;
Love unbearable grips our hearts,
We roar and yell without a scrap of embarrassment.

When the exultation digs in on our besotted hearts,
People mock us, as they listen to us speak,
Prattling without restraint of that which burns us up.

Exultation, Sweet Delight entering the mind!
Though the heart grow crafty in hiding its state,
It cannot forever hold from clamour.

Anyone who has not felt it will think you raving mad,
When they see you bewildered and bereft of sense:
But within your wounded heart, you care no whit for all
that lies without.

LAUD 77

Silent Love

SILENT LOVE, who do not wish to speak,
Hidden Love!

Love, hiding yourself throughout the seasons,
Who are never heard by those outside,
Whose treasure no thief
Knows how to rob!

The more one conceals you, the more your fire abounds:
The man who smothers you is scorched:
The man who battles against his longing to reveal you
Must suffer.

As for the man, even of high motive,
Who seeks to speak of you to others:
The wind comes gusting and sweeps away
All that he has.

If the one who has some light, whose candle flames,
Wants it to burn in peace, he must keep it hidden well.
He should close every door so that the wind does not blow in
And quench his spark.

Such love imposes silence on sighing,
Guarding all exits so that not a sigh escapes,
Making them parturient within, so that nothing of what is felt
Gets out.

If a sigh should escape, out follows the mind
And wanders, leaving what exists within behind.
When it repents, what is lost
Can never be found again.

This Love banishes all hypocrisy
From its realm.
Chases off vainglory
And all that might bolster it.

LAUD 81

The State of Love

LOVE, LOVE DIVINE, Love Unloved!

Your friendship, Love, is all delight.
The heart that has tasted you never sorrows more.

Loving Love, Consuming Love,
Love, sheltering the heart which gives you lodging!

Joyful Wound, Beloved Wound,
Wound thrilling the wounded one!

Love, where did you enter, passing so secretly in?
You left no sign to show your entry place.

Amiable, Delectable Love,
Love Inconceivable and Beyond Conception!

Love, Divine Fire; Playful, Laughing Love,
Never stinting, giving lavishly!

And with whom, Love, do you consort?
You put barons aside and go with the rejected.

To those valueless in others' eyes,
You give yourself lightly as though you gave but straw.

He, who would grasp you to widen his knowledge merely,
Will never feel or taste you in his heart.

Increase of knowledge only wounds
When not decked out with a humble heart.

Your doctrine, Lord, shapes desire.
You teach the gospel in pithy lessons.

Everburning Love, inflaming the hearts of your loved ones,
You make darts of their tongues that pierce to the pluck.

Gracious Love, Delectable Love,
Most Gentle Love, surfeiting the heart!

Love, you teach the way to eternity,
Providing a heavenly passport and a foretaste.

Love, Faithful Comrade, little recompensed,
Make me a pool of tears to weep for my sins.

Sweet, Gentle Love, Key of Heaven,
You lead the boats to haven and silence the storm.

Love, who give light to all that gives light,
The light we term Light is mere material light.

Illuming Light, Instructing Light,
Whoever is not lit by you can never know Love's plenitude

Love, you give light to the mind
And show there the object of Love's fullness.

Love, your ardour, inflaming the heart,
Unites it to Love Incarnate.

Love, Life Secure, Riches without Anxiety,
You last eternally and beyond our measuring.

Love, who give form to all that has form,
Let your Form reform all who are deformed.

Love, Pure and Clean; Love, Wise and Jocund,
You are profound and high in the heart that gives itself to you.

Generous, Courteous Love, those who trust in you
Can spend lavishly and keep a sumptuous table.

Fetid Lust leaves their minds,
They gleam of Chastity and are adorned with Freshness.

Divine Love, Medicine for every ailment, you cure the gravest ills.

Love, you are the hook that hooks me,
Hungry as I, your Beloved, am for your love.

ॐ

Insolent tongue, How dare you
Elevate yourself to speak of this state?

Think how you have spoken of Blessed Love
When every mouth must fail, describing it.

Even the angels in their choirs,
When they speak of Love just babble.

Have you no shame, reducing it all to words?
You praise not but blaspheme.

&

I cannot listen to your stricture never to speak of Love.
I will proclaim Love while I have breath.

No time should ever pass
When love is not proclaimed.

Heart and tongue call out, 'Love, O Love, O Love!'
If I should hide this sweetness, my very heart would burst.

For a heart that has tasted Love will crack
Or suffocate for want of shouting Love aloud.

LAUD 82

The Siege by Love

LOVE, O LOVE DIVINE,
Why have you laid siege to me?
You have fallen for me madly and cannot let me go.

From five directions you besiege me:
Through sight and hearing, taste and touch and smell.
If I emerge, I am caught: I cannot hide from you.

If I go out through my eyes, all I see is Love,
Depicted in every form, in every colour,
Reminding me over that I must live still with you.

If I go through the gate of hearing,
What does sound tell me? Sir, only of you.
I cannot exit here, for all I hear is bitter.

I cannot go through taste, since what I savour proclaims you:
Love, Love Divine! Love, Hungering Love,
You have hooked me that you might rule me!

If I go through the gate of smell,
Every creature has scent of you.
I return wounded, tangled in every odour.

If I go through the gate they call touch,
I trace you in every creature;
It is madness, Love, to try to escape you.

Love, I try to flee,
Not willing to yield my heart:
But I have lost, and cannot find, myself.

If I see evil in anyone, fault or weakness,
You transform me into them and make my heart heavy.
Love Immeasurable, who is it you choose for loving?

Take me, Dead Christ; haul me from sea to sand,
Where I may grieve to see you so full of wounds,
And why is it you have been wounded? Only that I be healed.

LAUD 83

The Crucifixion

SWEET LOVE, who have murdered your Love,
Slay me too, I beg, with love.

Love, was it for me,
That I might not perish,
That you led your own darling
To so cruel a death?
Do not pardon me then
Or permit me to escape death in Love's embrace.

Since you did not pardon your Beloved,
Why pardon me?
Show your love by hooking me
Like a fish, unable to break free.
Do not pardon me
For I long to drown in love.

Love hangs suspended: The cross holds him tightly
And will not let him go.
To save myself from madness,
I run to the cross and cling to it.
To flee would lead me to despair,
Wiped off from the roll of lovers.

O Cross, I fix and fasten myself to you
That, dying, I might taste life.
O Honeyed Death, savouring of life,
I am unhappy for want of your savour.
My Sweet, I burn to be wounded;
Let me die, heartbroken by love.

I run to the cross and read
Its bloodstained book,
This book that makes me
Doctor of Science and Philosophy.
O Book, you are gold within
And all aflower with love.

Love of the Lamb, broader than any sea,
Who can speak of you?
Only he who drowns himself in you
And knows not where he is,
To whom madness is the sanest way
As he wanders forward, crazed by Love.

LAUD 84

Madness

IT IS WISE AND SENSIBLE, it seems to me, to go quite mad
  for the Sweet Messiah

It is the very summit of wisdom to want to go mad for God:
No better philosophy is to be found, even in Paris.

The one who goes mad for Jesus seems full of affliction;
But he is the true doctor of life and theology.

The crowd will call you crazy if you go mad for Christ.
Never having felt the madness, they think you off your tree.

The one who would enter this school will find a new kind
  of learning:
Someone who never had this madness cannot comprehend it.

The one who would join this dance will find love without limit.
(May those who mock at him be pardoned!)

Those who thirst for status are not worthy of God's love:
Jesus himself, on the cross, hung between thieves.

But the one who seeks God by making himself foolish
  will quickly find Him:
He need never visit Bologna in search of novel teaching.

LAUD 85

A Meditation on Love

YOU, LOVE, WHO LOVE ME, grapple me with your hooks
That I may love as I am loved.

Love, who love but never find a worthy lover,
Whoever clambers in your branches is there without deserving.

O Noble Undeserving, to be caught up into the Most Admirable,
Knowing one could not rise at all did Love not lift one up!

Dynamic Love, failing to find a soul
Passive to the plenitude of Love Purified!

Love Without Plural, whose name is 'I Love',
Let me drink of the love gushing from your spring.

Let me see the 'How?' since the 'How Much?' is beyond me:
A quantity so immeasurable would swamp me.

   "The 'How?' I showed, becoming flesh:
   For you I was pilgrim, even to the cross.

   "The 'How Much?' depends on how you thirst,
   A high secret hidden from finite ones.

"The receiver, made by God from nothing,
Through no fault of the Giver, is insufficient.

"Infinite Love can show itself in finite things,
But the showing leads into Love Unlimited.

"In these abysses the saints are submerged,
Floundering in and out of the Love Unfathomable.

"Its height is infinite, its length immeasurable,
Its breadth impenetrable and vast.

"No greater demonstration could Love have given
Than to make myself the least and most despised of men,

"Who would be so mad as to make himself an ant
To save an ant army in their ant hill?

"My foolishness is greater: to come from my great height,
Take this road and suffer.

"My love was not for my benefit but yours:
I gained nothing for my pains.

"I am not increased by you or made less without you.
Love drew me towards you that you might be recreated.

"If you love me to gain glory, your love is a huckster's love
You attend my throne for what you can get.

"You attend with my price etched in your heart;
If the price falls, love fails.

"Your own interests are what drew you to love:
A little adversity and you find another object.

"If love is to be unavaricious and free,
The desire must be noble and without condition.

"There must be no limits, no self-interest
But real union, not dyed on like the stripes on a shirt.

"From such a love comes Love Marvellous,
Love that endures but ever stays the same".

LAUD 93

The Lament of Mary

"LADY OF PARADISE,
The Blessed Christ, your child, is taken.
Hurry, Lady, see how the crowd is flaying him:
They will surely finish him off, so harsh is their buffeting."

"How can this be, when he never did wrong?
Christ, My Hope! Why is he apprehended?"

"He is betrayed, Lady, sold by Judas
For thirty silver pieces; My, what a bargain!"

"Help, Magdalen, pain seizes me!
As was foretold, my son is being beaten."

"Help, Lady! Help! Now they spit on him.
The people push him forward: They hand him to Pilate."

"O Pilate, don't permit my son to be tormented:
I can show that he is maliciously accused."

"Crucify him! Crucify him! According to our law,
A man who makes himself king challenges the Senate."

"I beg you, hear me! Consider my sorrow!
Perhaps you can still go back on your decision."

"They are dragging out thieves for his companions.
Let him be crowned with thorns if he is king."

  "Son, Son, O Son! Son, Loving Lilyflower!
  Who, Son, will console my anguished heart?
  Son of the Laughing Eyes, Son, why don't you answer?
  Why do you spurn the breasts that suckled you?"

"Now the people bring the cross
On which the True Light will be uplifted."

  "What are you doing, Cross? Are you taking off my Son?
  What have you against him, who never did wrong?"

"Quick, Sorrowful Lady! Your son is stripped naked.
The crowd want him nailed to the wood."

  "Now they have torn off his clothes,
  Let me see how the cruel lash has bloodied him."

"Lady, they have taken his hand and stretched it on the cross.
With a nail they have pierced it: In this manner they have
        fixed it.
Now the second hand is taken: They spread it on the wood.
The pain increases, burning him up.
They take his feet now, Lady: They fix them to the tree,
Every limb outstretched, wrenching him all over."

  "I will begin my keening: My Son! My Comfort!
  Who is it who slays you, Delicate Child of Mine?
  They would have done me better service to have torn out
        my heart,
  Rather than stretch it on this cross."

"Mother, why are you here? You wound me to the quick.
Your lamentation overwhelms me, as I watch it take hold."

"Have I not cause enough, My Son? Son, Husband, Father,
Who is it who has stripped and injured you?"

"Mother, why do you keen, when I want you to remain,
To watch over these companions that I have won from the world?"

"Don't speak like that, Son! I want to die with you,
Never part from you till my last breath is drawn.
Let there be one burial place for us both, Son of a
        Doleful Mother.
Let them find us together, overcome by sorrow."

"With broken heart, My Mother, I place you with John.
He is my chosen: Call him your son."

"John, here is my mother: Take her for charity.
Pity her: Her heart is broken."

"Son, Son of the Forsaken Woman, Son of the Lifeless
        Woman,
Poisoned Son, your soul has gone from you.
Red Son and White Son, Son Incomparable,
To whom will I cling now you are gone?

"Fair Son and White Son, Son of the Merry Countenance,
Son, why does the world so despise you?"
Sweet Son and Darling Son, Son of the Grieving Mother,
Son, the people have treated you wickedly."

"John, New Son of Mine, your brother has died:
I have felt the knife that was foretold.
It has slain both son and mother. Callous death has seized us:
Let us be found in the end embracing, mother and son embracing."

LAUD 65

The Incarnation

LET US GO TO GIVE PRAISE and sing our acclaim
To the Love which has come to share itself as flesh.

Honour him, Beloved, who came to save you!
Quickly! Make no more delay in finding him!
He keeps nothing of himself that he will not give,
Since he wants to make you one with him.
How can you hold back and not give your all,
Taking him totally and embracing him lovingly?

Think how much he gives and what he wants back.
He does not require what you cannot give.
Sending no wealth before him,
He abandoned heaven and voyaged to earth.
He left a palace to stay in a stall
And with him brought no servant at all.

> "The seat of rich gold with gems resplendent,
> The brilliant crown, why did you leave them?
> The order of seraphim, the burning cherubim,
> The rejoicing court, why have you abandoned them?
> All those servants, all those maids
> Loved by you as brothers, why have you left them, Lord?

"Your throne so beautiful you have exchanged for a manger
And this bundle of straw whereon they place you.
For your garland of stars, you are swathed in sheets,
Cows and ass surround you who once had such honour.
You have Mary only beside you and Joseph
Who once were encircled by a court of glory.

"Were you drunk or out of your senses
To leave such a kingdom and so much riches?
Why did you give such a show of madness?
Had you a promise of higher majesty?
It surely points to a love beyond measure
To leave such a height for such little return.

"Well-bred Love, who is the object,
Wounding you so, driving you crazy?
You cannot deny you have given your all:
Something tremendous has clamped you tightly.
Such a love can lead but to death,
Giving no sign of lessening or cooling.

"Love so immeasurable has never been seen:
From your very birth, it has held its sway.
You were sold before you were born:
Love bought you and left back nothing.
You were sentenced to death for love,
Conquered by pain on a cross of suffering.

"Love made those conditions when first it wounded you,
Tearing everything from you with its powerful force,
It drew to itself your sense, your strength, your life
Like a magnet draws out iron.
You stooped down from your great height to baseness
And did not disdain stench and want.

"It is as if you did not understand
Or feel the abasement,
As if your light were darkened,
Your power and understanding lost.
You never defended yourself from the wound:
You surrendered strength and vigour.

"I know well that from early childhood
You had perfect knowledge and all power.
Tiny as you were, how did you contain
All your will in such vileness?
Great was your charity, to hide within yourself
Your wisdom strength and worth.

"In such vile clothes you wrapped yourself,
Making yourself needy and needing help.
Dear Wraps in which the High God
Bound himself as a destitute,
In which was clothed that treasure
That makes vile all gems and gold!"

How can one describe a love so immeasurable
As that which bound to itself the Omnipotent?
No love of father or son
Ever climbed to such a height,
Capturing so the mind, tying up all defences,
And letting itself be drawn beyond all sentience.

I can see that it is a father's nature to love a son
And a mother's to surrender him her very heart.
But I cannot conceive of them stripping themselves
Of strength and force and worth and giving him all.
A father can forgive himself for refusing to die
Or, even, suffer torment and grief for his beloved.

Who would give his life for love,
Retaining nothing to increase himself,
Purchase poverty with a precious pearl,
Sustain a mortal wound for it?
He who gives wants some exchange,
Wants the lover to love him as he loves.

"But what can a creature give you, Summit of Goodness,
For that which your charity gives him?
Since all his worth, compared to you,
Is less than dross, what can he give?
What can we give for your great benevolence?
Out of our unhealthiness can we bring delight?

"You have had, it seems, a vile recompense:
Does gold need tin to show off its beauty?
You have let yourself go mad for what return?
You have given up joy for our groans, wealth for our poverty.
Wasn't it crazy not to keep your sense and will,
In your eagerness to buy our love."

"Love, how great must be your power?
God's Majesty has abased itself for you.
You have wounded the heart of Love Supreme
So he might espouse our brutishness.
Crazy Jesus cannot cure himself:
Love makes him take pain as sweetness."

"Lovestruck God, talk to me of this love,
Which makes new and gives fresh joy to the lovers.
Could I but see your glorious face
I would repose myself there and need no more.
I want to hear how love captured you
To decide if I might acquire its ardour."

"My Spouse, whose question is my command,
Wonder at this bargain which Love has forced upon me:
Love makes me suffer,
Drawing me outside myself and nearer you.
Delay then no longer and yield yourself to me.
Take what I offer and offer me your heart.

"I am in love with you, Spouse of Mine.
Satisfy this yearning and take me as yours.
Love binds me, grasps me in its hook.
I call you 'Spouse', embrace you chastely.
To gain your love I stoop to you.
Love for you has caught me and burns me up.

"I leave wealth behind for you and choose to be poor,
Leave delight for suffering,
Change sweetness into adversity,
Tranquillity into affliction and need.
Acknowledge this perfect love
By giving love for love.

"You cannot give riches or talent,
Knowledge or ought else to increase me.
You have only yourself to pay me with.
You have nothing else of value to give back.
I am crazed for the love you can give.
The gift of your heart is what I ever seek.

"This is the trade I would make,
The gift of myself and all my wealth:
When I exchanged glory for bitter death,
I brought this treasure with me.
Take sweetness, return me pain:
Love unfailing makes me prodigal.

"I require little and give much.
I hold nothing back, in my longing to die for you.
If you consider my offer and my demand,
Will you refuse me what I ask?
Love, you have maddened me and I cannot stop myself,
I have lost more than any gambler.

"A bride gives a dowry but gets none back;
And gives it before the wedding day.
No man is foolish enough to give a dowry
Unless the woman is so exalted
And of such high parentage
That she would raise him in dignity and station.

"I seek no grandeur or ennobling
From you, O Spouse, to whom I give myself.
I take on want for you, shame and servitude.
Love me then forever.
I demand no dowry but offer one:
All my blood poured painfully upon a cross.

"For dowry, I will give you riches immeasurable,
Beyond desire or dream,
Held for you in Heaven
Where it can never be plundered or perish.
You will be dressed in light, brighter than the sun,
After you are stripped of fault and stench.

"With a crown of stars, you will be crowned,
Placed on a throne of gems and gold,
Your clothes worked with diamond and pearl.
Your room will be decked with drapes and baldachin.
You will be made all divine. (I speak in figures:
You cannot conceive such splendour).

"To give you such state, I have come to this,
Repose myself in a filthy stall.
Repay, then, love of such magnitude,
Bearing so much wealth and such delight.
Let not your heart linger
But let your mind take fire and fervently embrace my love.

"I beg you to give me love, My Spouse.
I ask for nothing else.
Love shows no pity, stripping me bare.
It has bound me tightly and never ceases its burning.
Spouse, so beloved, give me your love.
I have paid for you dearly and cannot give more."

"Jesus, beloved Spouse, tell me what I can do,
So I might love you as much as I ought.
You did not think it a trial to suffer for me.
You wanted to save me, who had had fallen into fault."
(Look! For me Divine Majesty has come
To make of a servant a queen, drawing me from all my stench!)

"I am all yours, Love, who created me,
Then redeemed me when I was condemned to die.
He who finds what he has lost
Guards it more securely and loves it more deeply.
None but you has any rights to me, O Christ.
You made the purchase: yours it is to guard.

"If I could give you more than all myself, I would:
But I have nothing more.
If I had the world and all its produce
And more besides, I would give my very life to you.
I'd give with all my heart, my power, my will,
My hope, my love and my desire.

"It is no equal exchange but it is all you ask.
I give what you command, a will infinite
And unlimited that will not stray elsewhere
Or spread itself about, but wraps itself in you.
Love, you have wounded my heart. If it could die
And have a thousand other lives, it would give them all
    to you.

"Do you demand your bride give more,
Who longs so dearly to embrace you?
Sweet Life of Mine, do not make me suffer
But give me your gracious face to contemplate.
If you could not defend yourself from love yourself,
How can I fight back against its heat?

"Pity me then, Merciful Jesus.
Do not ever leave me without you, My Spouse.
When you withhold your love from me,
I weep and wail and almost die.
When you divorce yourself from me, you are cruel.
The world and all its sweetness is bitter.

"Now I must sing, for my Love is born.
He has redeemed me and has given me his ring.
Love, come as flesh, burns me so.
I embrace him who is my brother."
"O Darling Child, I have conceived you in my heart
And hold you in my arms, crying out, 'Love'."

"I invite you, Lovers, to this wedding,
So joyous and sweet, for love is here.
He unites himself to us with all his amorous riches.
Where he is, there is sweet delight."

"Sweetheart, you are made new: Embrace the Spouse,
Who gives you every joy. Let us shout. 'Love, O my Love!'

"Keep us, Love, drunk on love,
Let us stay wrapped in you, transformed into love.
Watch that we be not led astray
But let us stay always in love, with hearts upraised forever.
You were born for us, O Love: Sate us with that love
That Pharisee or Scribe can never taste or quaff."

Printed in the United Kingdom
by Lightning Source UK Ltd.
127597UK00001B/82-90/A

9 781904 556862